We Need
Mail Carriers

by Lola M. Schaefer

Consulting Editor: Gail Saunders-Smith, Ph.D.

Consultant: Gery Schneider, Postmaster,
United States Postal Service

Pebble Books

an imprint of Capstone Press
Mankato, Minnesota

Pebble Books are published by Capstone Press
818 North Willow Street, Mankato, Minnesota 56001
http://www.capstone-press.com

Library of Congress Cataloging-in-Publication Data
Schaefer, Lola M., 1950–
    We need mail carriers/by Lola M. Schaefer.
    p. cm.—(Helpers in our community)
    Includes bibliographical references and index.
    Summary: Simple text and photographs describe mail carriers and their role in
our communities.
    ISBN 0-7368-0392-0
    1. Letter carriers—United States juvenile literature. 2. Letter carriers—Juvenile
literature. [1. Letter carriers.] I. Title. II. Series: Schaefer, Lola M., 1950– Helpers in
our community.
HE6499.S32 2000
383'.143'0973—dc21   99-19433
                                                                                          CIP

Note to Parents and Teachers

The Helpers in Our Community series supports national social studies standards for units related to community helpers and their roles. This book describes and illustrates mail carriers and how they help people. The photographs support early readers in understanding the text. The repetition of words and phrases helps early readers learn new words. This book also introduces early readers to subject-specific vocabulary words, which are defined in the Words to Know section. Early readers may need assistance to read some words and to use the Table of Contents, Words to Know, Read More, Internet Sites, and Index/Word List sections of the book.

Table of Contents

Mail carriers work for the post office.

PROPERTY OF U.S. POSTAL SERVICE

UNITED STATES
POSTAL SERVICE

6

Mail carriers pick up mail from mailboxes.

Mail carriers bring this mail to the post office.

Mail carriers sort mail by address.

12

Mail carriers pick up mail for their routes.

Some mail carriers walk their routes.

7206856

ONE WAY

3913

72

GRUMMAN

U.S.MAIL

T.P. 50

16

Some mail carriers drive their routes.

Mail carriers deliver mail to businesses.

Mail carriers deliver mail to homes.

Words to Know

address—the number and street of a business or home; mail carriers in the United States deliver mail to more than 130 million addresses every day.

deliver—to bring something to someone; mail carriers in Canada deliver mail to more than 12 million addresses every day.

mail—letters, cards, and packages sent through a post office

post office—a government building where people go to buy stamps and send letters and packages; the United States has 38,019 post offices.

route—a set path that mail carriers follow to deliver mail; mail carriers walk or drive their routes.

sort—to arrange or separate things into groups; mail carriers sort mail by address to make delivery easier.

Read More

Berger, Melvin and Gilda. *Where Does the Mail Go?* Discovery Readers. Philadelphia: Chelsea House Publishers, 1998.

Greene, Carol. *Postal Workers Deliver Our Mail.* Plymouth, Minn.: The Child's World, 1998.

Ready, Dee. *Mail Carriers.* Community Helpers. Mankato, Minn.: Bridgestone Books, 1998.

Internet Sites

Canada Post
http://www.canadapost.ca

Smithsonian National Postal Museum
http://www.si.edu/postal

United States Postal Service
http://www.usps.gov/kids

Index/Word List

Word Count: 61
Early-Intervention Level: 6

Editorial Credits
Karen L. Daas, editor; Abby Bradford, Bradfordesign, Inc., cover designer; Kimberly Danger, photo researcher

Photo Credits
David F. Clobes, 6, 12, 18
Index Stock Imagery/David Lissy, cover; Aneal Vohra (1995), 4; Jeff Dunn, 20; Zane Williams (1990), 14
Leslie O'Shaughnessy, 8, 10
Photri-Microstock/Brent Jones, 1; MacDonald Photography, 16